Viol...in
th...

The Practicing Administrator's Leadership Series
Jerry J. Herman and Janice L. Herman, Editors

**ROADMAPS
TO SUCCESS**

Other Titles in This Series Include:

Violence in the Schools

How to Proactively Prevent and Defuse It

Joan L. Curcio
Patricia F. First

CORWIN PRESS, INC.
A Sage Publications Company
Newbury Park, California

For information address:

Corwin Press, Inc.
A Sage Publications Company
2455 Teller Road
Newbury Park, California 91320

SAGE Publications Ltd.
6 Bonhill Street
London EC2A 4PU
United Kingdom

SAGE Publications India Pvt. Ltd.
M-32 Market
Greater Kailash I
New Delhi 110 048 India

Printed in the United States of America

Library of Congress Cataloging-in-Publication Data

Curcio, Joan L.
    Violence in the schools: how to proactively prevent & defuse it /
Joan L. Curcio, Patricia F. First.
        p.   cm. — (Roadmaps to success)
    Includes bibliographical references (p.)
    ISBN 0–8039–6058–1
    1. School violence—United States—Prevention. 2. Students—
United States—Crimes against.   I. First, Patricia F.   II. Title.
III. Series
    LB3013.3.C87   1993
    371.7′82—dc20   93-22348

93 94 95 96 10 9 8 7 6 5 4 3 2 1

Corwin Press Production Editor: Marie Louise Penchoen

Contents

Foreword

In *Violence in the Schools: How to Proactively Prevent and Defuse It,* Joan L. Curcio and Patricia F. First explore the wide range of violence that is occurring in our schools. They address the categories of student-to-student violence, student-to-teacher violence, and teacher-to-student violence and consider the ever-present overtones of racial and ethnic conflict.

The major causes of violence in the school community—both in and out of schools—are identified, and suggestions are offered for dealing with such causes as well as their results. Commonsense actions are outlined to answer each specific type of violence. Although this is primarily a useful guidebook for administrators and teachers to successfully confront violent situations in their schools, this book also deals heavily with prevention and intervention strategies.

Curcio and First provide practical suggestions to all persons who are involved in defusing violence in schools. Indeed, their work serves as a useful resource and guidebook for all aspects of this serious problem.

JERRY J. HERMAN
JANICE L. HERMAN
Series Co-Editors

About the Authors

Joan L. Curcio is Associate Professor in the Department of Educational Leadership, University of Florida, where she researches and writes on education law. She has had extensive experience as a school practitioner: teacher, assistant principal, high school principal, and assistant superintendent. She was named among the 100 Top Administrators in North America in 1984 by the National School Boards Association for her work as principal. Curcio received her Ph.D. from Virginia Polytechnic and State University and presently teaches higher education law, public school law, special education law, and the superintendency.

Patricia F. First is Professor of Educational Law and Policy in the Department of Educational Leadership & Policy Studies at the University of Oklahoma, where she conducts policy studies in education related to justice for children. She is the author of *Educational Policy for School Administrators*, the co-editor of *School Boards: Changing Local Control*, and the author of numerous articles in policy and practitioner journals. She has been a teacher and administrator in both K-12 and higher education, a policy analyst with both state and federal government, and a National Education Policy Fellow.

Introduction:
Danger Zone or Haven?

It may turn out that a free society cannot really prevent crime. Perhaps its causes are locked so deeply into the human personality, the intimate processes of family life, and the subtlest aspects of the popular culture that coping is the best that we can hope to do. But we don't know that yet.

(WILSON, 1992)

The Presence of Violence

In 1991, a report of the Federal Bureau of Investigation confirmed statistically what school administrators had already guessed, that violent crimes by juveniles of ages 10-17 had ballooned during the 1980s and still surge upward in the 1990s. These crimes are carried out by children who represent different social classes, lifestyles, races, and geographic areas of the country (Lawton, 1992). They bring their weapons, drugs, grudges, problems, anger, and potential for danger to school with them when they come. They mingle there with other children—some who skirt on the edge of danger themselves and some who have been victims rather than perpetrators of violence, both inside and outside the school gates.

As a consequence, parents from all kinds of neighborhoods worry about whether or not their children will come home safe. Teachers as well have concerns about safety in their own classrooms. Children fear being in isolated areas of the school, or being alone without their friends at certain times and places. For many, the symbol of the little red schoolhouse as a safe haven has been replaced by the yellow and black sign, Danger Zone.

As educators, we are reluctant to acknowledge the presence of violence in our environment, either to external parties or to each other. The reasons are multiple. First of all, there's an unfortunate tendency to accept certain aberrant behavior as normal for children. Fighting, for example, or boys teasing and harassing girls about their bodies is perceived as "just part of growing up" rather than a prelude to much more dangerous and violent behavior. And then, there is nostalgia for the old days when the worst discipline problem administrators handled was class cutting. There's denial, also, that anything could be wrong "in our school"—those are things that happen "downtown." Of course there's reluctance, and certainly fear, in confronting the violence that can come with gang activity, drug dealing, and guns. No wonder we are reluctant. We were trained to operate schools—not danger zones. The nature and extent of violent behavior that occurs on campus today is constantly changing and increasing. Strategies and guidelines and policies are needed to help school officials fulfill their responsibility to provide a safe and healthy school environment.

The Scope of the Problem in Schools

Television and newspapers report daily the incidence of violence in and around schools: A gunman kills and wounds children in an elementary school playground; a student stabs a teacher in the back; a gang of boys rape a high school girl in the school storage closet; a student shoots an administrator in the school corridor; racial slurs and threats are written on the school's outside wall. In

1989, a survey of inner-city 6th- and 8th-graders showed that more than 50% of them had had money and/or personal property stolen, some more than once; 32% had carried a weapon to school; and 15% had hit a teacher during the year (Menacker, Weldon & Hurwitz, 1989). And these figures don't reflect the numbers of youth who come to school *already* violated physically, sexually, emotionally, or negligently; nor do they include those who are harmed on their way to or from school.

The Scope of the Problem Outside Schools

Schoolchildren are in even greater danger of confronting violence outside the school. Particularly in urban neighborhoods surrounding schools, although not exclusively, the threat of theft, assault, vandalism, and shootings is serious, and students (as well as teachers) are frightened and wary. Add to this the fact that many children do not have to leave home to experience the cold grip of violence. Considerable numbers of them see their fathers beat their mothers, sisters, and brothers; they witness rapes, stabbings, and murders; they are sexually abused; and even in the "finest" of homes, they are traumatized through emotional and psychological neglect.

The Responsibility for Safe Schools

It is not contradictory then to say that despite the presence of violence and the threat to personal safety that hovers over schools, schools are still, for many children, the safest place in their lives. The notion that schools should be safe havens is a concept that has found support in law throughout the history of public schools— for teachers to teach and children to learn, there must be a safe and inviting educational environment.

Recently, however, that message has been underscored. California, for instance, has amended its constitution to read that schoolchildren and school staff members have an inalienable right to safe and peaceful schools, and its high court recognized a "heightened responsibility" for school officials in charge of children and their school environments. Numerous legislatures and courts, in the past 5 to 10 years in fact, have addressed the presence of violent behavior in the schools and noted what responsibility school officials have for the maintenance of schools where education can occur, and they have spoken of the challenge of restoring order and discipline. Although it is tempting to view courts as intrusive in school matters, they often simply are issuing reminders that all students have a right to be safe, unvictimized, and unabused at school. However, the courts also recognize that in order to fulfill their duty to maintain an orderly learning environment, teachers and administrators must have broad supervisory and disciplinary powers. This book addresses the effective use of those powers in the face of violent behaviors. Although the challenges of supervision are great today, and sometimes even overwhelming, people working in schools can access the skills, strategies, and resources that will empower them to create a safe and nurturing school environment. In the pages that follow, we recommend many strategies that are known to be the most useful and successful.

The Structure of This Book

Violence in schools is a complex issue. Students assault teachers, strangers harm children, students hurt each other, and any one of the parties may come to school already damaged or violated. The kind of violence an individual encounters varies also, ranging from mere bullying to rape or murder.

To ensure the reader easy access to information on a specific problem, we have divided this book into chapters on the basis of who is being violent to whom—for example, student-to-student violence—followed by a chapter on violence-prevention strategies and a chapter on what to do in an actual crisis. Each category chapter also has specific information on prevention and crisis issues, and the reader will find that many of the recommendations we make are appropriate to more than one perpetrator-victim category.

It is important to acknowledge here that much of the violence discussed in the following chapters as school problems is actually a reflection of the social, economic, and political problems of the larger American society. The need, for example, for gun safety awareness programs for children in schools grows from the combination of the reluctance of the country to date to choose the policy option of national gun control, of bored and unattended children, and of a host of related issues. It is also acknowledged that the impetus for violence can stem from attitudes, beliefs, and conflicts that originate outside the school but erupt in that setting—emotional feelings concerning religious beliefs, racial and cultural hatred, censorship, and homophobia, for example. Such broad causes exceed the scope of this book; however, we will look briefly, in Chapter 7, at attitudes and values of educators and their potential impact on the decrease of violence.

An administrator's roadmap to success regarding the presence or absence of violence in school begins with the next chapter. Coping is *not* the best that we can do.

Student-to-Student Violence

When violence erupts at school, the major actors often are students harming other students. In fact, administrators sometimes mark the passing of a semester or year by the number of violent incidents that have transpired between students. When a superintendent of a moderately sized school district in the Southwest was asked how the past school semester went, she said, "Not as well as I'd have liked it to. We had a drug-related shooting, a student stabbing, and a family incident in which a father shot and killed the mother and then himself." She followed that comment with this one, "And ours is a 'good' district."

Two of those three incidents involved students, and being a "good" school district did not keep it immune from violent acts perpetrated by its student occupants. Dysfunctional children, from dysfunctional families, are found in schools and communities of all shapes and sizes, and unfortunately their hostility, anger, frustration, and danger to themselves or others are not always apparent. What we are sure of is that, increasingly, children experience isolation and alienation at home and at school and are lonely, desperate, and callously victimizing each other.

The Roots of Violence

Although it is not possible within the purview of this book to examine the roots of violent acts of students, it is important to identify and comment on them. For without some clues, we are helpless to develop strategies, anticipate trouble, or prevent injury.

When Menacker, Weldon, and Hurwitz (1989) speak of the breakdown of order and the presence of violence in schools as community issues, they hit the mark. The most urgent issue for improving conditions, they suggest, is addressing the social pathology of the communities in which schools are located. Beyond the "get-tough" measures, which help for the short term in specific circumstances, is a need for interventions developed from an understanding of community and family conditions. In poor urban settings that are stressed by economic deprivation, children live in neighborhood projects where violent crimes occur regularly and are witnessed by the children, and where the perpetrators and/or victims are known to them. Children too are victimized there, not only by abuse but by an onslaught of psychological, emotional, and social assaults born of poverty, denigration, neglect, and lack of respect. In middle- and upper-class settings, the conditions are not so dramatic, but some children still experience violent behavior.

Listen to a highly respected principal of East Harlem whose student was accused of taking part in the rape and attack on a Central Park jogger. "Violence is normal in the world of today's adolescent. . . . From Rambo to the corporate raiders, it's the aggressive, tough-minded guys who get the job done regardless of laws and the societal constraints. . . . They're the admirable, effective people" (Flax, 1989, p. 13). The difference between middle-class/working-class and poor children, she suggests, is that the former sees cruelty as necessary temporary conformity and the latter sees it as the way the world is.

There is nothing simple about why students harm each other, but there are some clues. Consider neglect, dysfunctional conditions within families, medical insults and traumas, and societal devaluation and exploitation of children. Add to that what children learn at very early ages about power and how it is acquired. Consider the modeling many children experience at home and in the community. A commitment to finding constructive ways to proactively prevent and defuse violence in the schools in the face of these problems is necessary, as well as a belief that it can be done in a respectful way.

How Students Harm Each Other

Before preventing or curtailing violent behavior in schools is discussed, it is important to be clear about what violence is in that setting. Because the teaching/learning process is the focus there, and the adults in the building stand *in loco parentis*, any behavior that violates, damages, or abuses peers has to be of concern—middle-school boys grabbing girls in inappropriate places, for example. To establish a common base of violent behaviors and potentially violent behaviors, the following categories are listed. This list is not fully inclusive, and some may disagree with where each item has been placed, but it offers a framework of student-to-student violence from which to discuss administrative strategies for preventing or defusing student violence.

Gravely Serious, Violent Acts of Students

- Suicide
- Rape, Murder, Drive-by shootings
- Firing a gun in a crowded school corridor
- Possession of weapons on school property
- Stabbing fatally or wounding
- Hate crimes

Serious Violent Acts of Students

- Sexual assault
- Extortion
- Vandalism of each other's property
- Interracial incidents
- Drug dealing and drug abuse

Potentially Serious and Violent Behavior

- Fistfighting
- Taunting and intimidation
- Boys slapping and mistreating girlfriends
- Bullying younger and weaker peers
- Gang membership and gang activity
- Wearing gang identification
- Boys teasing and harassing girls
- Use of alcohol in school
- Group hazing
- Property/theft disputes

Stopping Student Violence Before It Gets Started

When violence first became an issue with which administrators had to deal, they found themselves preoccupied with each incident, each crisis, and with no time to reflect on what they did that worked, or didn't work, to defuse the situation. As it became apparent that schools and children were changing with a more transient, materialistic society that was also less family-oriented, homogeneous, and more violent, administrators learned to manage crises but not necessarily to prevent them. Today we know that the safety and welfare of schoolchildren depend on the ability of school officials to foresee and to prevent dangerous situations where one student is a threat to another. But where do we begin?

The road to success is built piece by piece. In order to implement a plan to reduce and prevent violence among students in a school or school district, we must have several fundamental pieces to begin with. Any plan will have the best chance of success when the following six building blocks are in place.

1. A Shared System of Beliefs and Values

Of primary importance is that school and school district staffs, in collaboration with the larger school community, spend time and energy examining their personal beliefs and values regarding schools and children, sharing them, and working toward a common set of beliefs to which everyone can consistently subscribe. How success-fully people working in a school can influence the behavior of stu-dents and preserve the school as a safe place is affected by what these workers value and believe. It would be helpful for a staff to explore its values regarding fundamental fairness, individual re-sponsibility, the right to a respectful existence, parental involve-ment, and cooperation versus competition. Beliefs regarding how students learn and acquire discipline, knowledge, motivation, or self-worth will set the stage for developing the vision of a school or school district.

2. A Vision of Respect

Part of the process of formulating a comprehensive philosophy and vision that the whole school can accept and live by is identify-ing what is acceptable and unacceptable behavior. Involve the whole school community in developing a vision of respect for each other, one that articulates expectations and recognizes the individual's right to a peaceful existence at school and a nurturing environment of learning. It is necessary to believe with Roland Barth (1990) that "the character and quality of schools will dramat-ically improve when, and if, those who work in schools—teachers, students, parents, and administrators—come in touch with one an-other, with their personal visions, and with the way they would like their schools to be, and then take deliberate steps to move to-ward them" (p. 158). Although it is not within the power of school personnel to control the cultural and social environment outside the school, it is within the power of the school community to build its own cultural biases toward respect, learning, and the absence of violence in the school setting.

3. Explicit Policies

Definite policies regarding rights, responsibilities, expectations, and consequences must be formulated.

Begin with putting on paper the district's and school's *commit-ment to proactivity,* and to handling every incident as it arises so that no violent or potentially violent behavior is ignored. Research shows that administrators tend to put energy into minor disciplinary incidents that are more easily resolved because of the strain on resources required by more difficult cases that involve expulsion or police reports (Menacker, Hurwitz, & Weldon, 1990). Provide in policy for *a code of student conduct* that will be disseminated and clearly understood by all. Describe in writing the procedures that will be followed when a critical incident threatens or occurs. Particular policies need to be formulated regarding *support of the victim* in the aftermath of the violence. Where the school community supports and places its sympathies with the victim, it sends a message of intolerance to violent behavior; sensitivity to the difficulties and sufferings of the victim strengthens the culture of the school. Be specific about the logical *consequences of harmful and disruptive behavior*. Address the fear that violent acts engender directly, starting with trust-building that begins before the violence occurs. One of the ways trust among the school community can be developed is through the next item.

4. A Holistic Plan of Staff Development

For unity in the enforcement of both the letter and the spirit of the formulated policies, a holistic plan should be developed. A complete plan would include strategies of prevention and intervention, designed to assist the staff in helping to avert violent acts. It would include strategies for coping with incidents of violence and tragedy as and after they occur. An effective staff development program that emphasizes the safety and welfare of the school community is one that fosters adult interdependence and strategy sharing, encourages practice, and involves time and follow-up. One-shot workshops will not develop the commitment and trust that is important to a staff who are determined to share responsibility for the safety and welfare of themselves and their students.

Each school community knows its own staff development needs best. Confront the difficult areas first, by planning to examine those issues that most directly impact the school or district. There are endless possibilities: hate crimes, racial and cultural violence, the role and stance of security guards, attitudes toward weapons and gun safety awareness programs, gangs and gang activity, abuse identification, and troublesome political symbolism, such as the display of the Confederate flag.

5. District Statements of Policy

Specific public statements from the district regarding the accepted policies—for instance, that racism and/or discrimination will not be tolerated or condoned—will demonstrate unity and determination and reinforce the desired "culture" of the schools.

6. The Use of Learned Strategies

Employing learned strategies can both prevent and defuse violence in the schools. These strategies for all kinds of violence and specifically for student-to-student issues are discussed in Chapter 5. Strategies for other categories of violence are discussed in Chapters 3 and 4.

In Summary

We have seen here how preparation is necessary before addressing not only student-to-student violence but all types of violence encountered in the schools. School officials cannot simply rush in with hard rules and heavy hands. The way must be prepared with understanding, cooperation, and planning. Violence in the schools is a serious and growing problem, but it can be handled, prevented, and perhaps dissipated if only the school officials do not become themselves part of the problem.

Student-to-Teacher Violence

No teacher who has worked in the school environment longer than 5 years has to check the statistics in order to know that the number of attacks on teachers and administrators by students (and in some cases, by students' parents) are on the rise. As early as 1978, a study sponsored by the Department of Health, Education, and Welfare on safe schools and violent schools uncovered disturbing facts about the presence of danger and disruption. *Specifically, it was discovered that 12% of the teachers surveyed reported having been threatened* with physical harm every month and admitted to being reluctant to confront disruptive students. Half of all the teachers surveyed had also experienced verbal abuse. When a similar study was done 20 years later with Chicago teachers and students, the increase in assaults against teachers, as well as their present vulnerable positions, were clear: Students admitted hitting teachers at least once, sometimes twice, during the year; *a small percentage of teachers said they were actually physically attacked or threatened with a weapon,* and a large percentage said their personal property had been damaged or stolen at school (Menacker, Weldon, & Hurwitz, 1989). Although the incidence of assaults on educators is affected by a number of variables, such as grade levels, size of district, geography, and even the level of community respect for teachers, it is widespread. Anyone working in schools could be a victim of violent behavior.

Martha: A Brief Case Story

From one of the authors' school administrative experience comes this brief case story of Martha, a genteel, good-humored, and talented high school English teacher whose high academic standards were softened by her charming Southern accent and her sensitivity to the needs of students. She taught two classes of "honor" students and two classes of "basic" students in a suburban school that had recently been rural. The geographic area of the school, just 25 miles from a growing metropolitan area, was exploding with population. One morning, during her planning period, as she was walking through the second-floor corridor near her classroom, she saw Lenny, one of her "basic" students, at his locker. He furtively stuffed things into his locker when he spotted her and stood clutching his coat and glaring at her as she approached.

Martha was concerned. She and Lenny had been through a lot together, and she believed that she had influenced him positively to achieve in her class. They had "a good thing going," and she wanted to reinforce that. "Lenny, what's going on? You're supposed to be in class right now, aren't you ?" "Don't hassle me, old lady, I got something to do; get out of my way!" Martha reached out to put her hand on Lenny's arm in a gesture of caring. He shoved her against the lockers with force enough to knock her down. She fell, her arm hitting the ground first, as Lenny ran at top speed out of the building. Martha cried out for help, and one of the administrators found her on the corridor floor.

Many appropriate things were done. Martha was taken to a hospital emergency room and treated; she had bruises, aches, and pains, and her elbow was broken. The assault was reported to the police. Martha was encouraged to bring assault and battery charges against Lenny. She never did. The school officials called Lenny's home and asked his parents to come to the school with Lenny, where appropriate school action would be determined. They never came and Lenny never returned to school. Martha was comforted by her close colleagues when she returned after more than a month's absence. The incident had been described at a faculty meeting, and procedures on how to approach students in the hall during instructional time were discussed. Hall supervision was increased. Martha's immediate supervisor at school called her regularly during her absence to see how she was progressing. Martha's was the first incident of teacher assault in this school, and not much was known about victimization or its effects in this setting. When Martha returned, she was subdued and much less eager to stay after class with her students. She went directly to the teachers' lounge at the beginning of her planning period and stayed there until her next class began. She attended only required extracurricular activities. The next year Martha was gone, retiring at the first opportunity.

What Can Be Done?

A first response is *training, training, training*. One set of skills for people working in schools that will hold the entire school district in good stead is *conflict resolution*. Not all physical confrontation can be avoided in the school environment, but the ability to defuse violent behavior and to keep an incident from deteriorating into a physical attack is a valuable one. Schools and school districts have a responsibility to provide staff development in crisis prevention strategies, in dealing with disruptive children, and in mediating conflict. School employees should be encouraged to attend seminars and workshops in these strategies, given release time, and asked to share their skills or knowledge with the whole faculty.

As Houston and Grubaugh (1989) make clear, administrators and teachers hold a special place in the school and the classroom as authority figures. In the perspective of students, school officials are exercising their power daily, and consequently any perceived or actual abuse of that power can bring quick retaliation. They can either be targets of direct student aggression or be scapegoats of violence intended for someone else (a girlfriend or an abusive father). Teachers need to know that this can happen and need to be given the opportunity to gain communication skills that assist them in dealing with these situations. Teacher education programs share in the responsibility for producing young teachers who have learned these skills and strategies and who have had opportunities to practice them.

A second response is to support more *policies and legislation that are protective* of the school employee. In monitoring legislation, the school community needs to keep a watchful eye on the reduction of staff, as budget issues cut further and further into school operations. Fewer adults in the building means less and sparser supervision, leaving many school employees to play solitary supervisory roles and thereby to become easier targets for violent attacks.

A third response is *the creation of a school culture and sense of community* in which those who work in a school take responsibility for each other and depend on each other. An environment in which isolation and/or alienation among the teachers and administration exists is ripe for victimization. Buddy systems, pairing new teachers with experienced teachers, and collaborative projects contribute to a sense of respect and unity that is visible to the entire community.

A fourth response is to have *a plan for emergencies* with which every school employee is familiar.

A fifth response is to understand that a school's responsibility to provide a safe setting where teaching and learning occurs means that *reasonable precautions must be taken regarding the safety of staff as well as that of students.* The school district cannot be negligent in that regard. Be security conscious in protecting employees from violence. Where employees work in remote areas—an office in the gymnasium, a reading lab in a temporary hut or trailer, in an auto body shop, or in places separated from the main building, especially before and after hours—it is important that these areas be well-lit, secure, and equipped to send emergency communications, if necessary. *Where the school neighborhood is known as a violent one, or a staff member has been threatened directly, or a rape or stabbing or other violent incident has occurred, or a school employee has concerns regarding safety due to negligent conditions at the school, there is a greater duty for protection.*

Asking the following questions and acting on the answers will increase the safety from assault of not only teachers but students as well:

- Are certain areas where employees work too obscured for normal supervision?
- Can these areas be modified, redesigned, or made more visible—by landscaping, for instance?
- Can certain offices where employees work late or early be moved closer to the front office (Gerl, 1991)?

Many of the preventive measures included in Chapter 5 on student-to-student violence work toward reducing student-to-teacher violence as well. However, the most helpful strategies from that chapter appropriate to the reduction of teacher assault are those included under the plan to reduce and prevent violence.

Supporting Teachers Through the Crisis

The Use of Force as a Defense

When attacks are made on teachers, administrators, and others working in the school, the law permits them to defend themselves (and others) with reasonable force necessary to prevent physical harm. Florida, for instance, has a law that makes it a crime to assault a school employee who is on school property. Even states that have discarded corporal punishment as a disciplinary measure have passed laws that allow educators to protect themselves and others from assault (Henderson, Golanda, & Johnson, 1989).

School officials need to know that using force against a student who is attacking them is acceptable as a defense in the courts. The key words are *necessary* and *reasonable*. If the force far exceeds what is necessary—given, for instance, the relative size and strength of the attacking student, as opposed to that of the teacher—then the force will not be sanctioned; nor will it be sanctioned if it comes after the attacker has been subdued or disarmed. Of course, if the teacher is not in the situation of self-defense but rather in the defense of another student or adult, the standard of *necessary* and *reasonable* force would be the same. Finally, there is the expectation that if the teacher had time to seek assistance from the principal or other administrators and security personnel, that would be done before force was employed in self-defense (Henderson, Golanda, & Johnson, 1989).

Actions That Can Be Taken

1. Where there are not specific state laws protecting school employees from assault, attackers can be prosecuted for assault and battery or juvenile delinquency under state criminal laws. Damages also may be sought in civil suits for assault and battery. Check to see if school board policies offer some recourse to the victim employee; they should at least stipulate disciplinary actions to be taken against the attacker (Zirkel & Gluckman, 1991). Good advice from two education law experts follows:

   Schools and their employees are not at all immune to violence. Administrators can help protect themselves and their fellow employees by vigorously pressing criminal charges and assisting with civil suits for assault and battery. At the same time, they must be vigilant about school security with regard to facilities, staffing, and practices. (Zirkel & Gluckman, 1991, p. 106)

2. Call the police when an attack on a teacher occurs.
3. Advise the battered teacher to seek the advice of an attorney.
4. Take appropriate school disciplinary actions, following board policies regarding students assaulting teachers.
5. Squelch rumors throughout the school and community through direct and immediate communication (see also recommended actions to be taken in the event of racial/ethnic conflict and the use of guns and other weapons in Chapter 6).

Supportive Actions

How the teacher victim is treated following the incident will affect the entire school for a long time after. Victims of criminal assaults experience powerlessness, depression, and even guilt and shame. It is crucial to their recovery and to the school's recovery that they not be victimized further. School administrative actions that are supportive include the following:

• Assigning school personnel to stay with the victim immediately after the incident and until family or friends arrive.

- Forming a support cadre to maintain contact throughout recovery until the employee returns to school; the principal or other supervisor makes clear that the victim's well-being is of primary concern.
- Apprising the victim of what actions for remedying the harm can be taken.
- Informing the victim of employee benefits, such as workman's compensation.
- The school district not inflicting further harm on the teacher through blame or recrimination.
- Referring the victim to a counseling program, especially one that specifically addresses trauma.
- Giving the victim, where possible, access to legal services for attacks on school grounds.

In Summary

Martha, the teacher who was assaulted by one of her students in this chapter's brief case story, was neither trained to avoid or handle the kind of confrontation that led to her assault and victimization nor sufficiently supported after the incident to regain her confidence or sense of control and to remain in the classroom. There is an obligation today, given the potential for violent occurrences in schools, to prepare school employees to anticipate and handle such incidents. There is an equal obligation to assist those who have been victimized to deal with their sense of vulnerability and betrayal, to overcome their fears, and to restore themselves as whole persons again. Teacher assaults must not be minimized or trivialized in order to protect the reputation of the school or school district. Rather, every legal means against the assailant should be pursued. Causing the attacker to face the consequences of violent behavior and giving the victim full and caring support send powerful messages out from the school community.

Teacher-to-Student Violence

Teachers and administrators stand *in loco parentis* to students and are entrusted with their care during the time that they are in school. In general, this trust is valued and honored; when it is broken, as it has been, there is not only a moral but also a legal cost. As Ralph Mawdsley says:

> Elementary and secondary school students who are subject to the state's compulsory attendance requirements and who have not reached the age of legal majority are, in a sense, entrusted to schools. So, courts may regard the relationship between students and school employees as a special one, and may hold school employees to a higher standard of care under the common law than are many other employees. (Mawdsley, 1992, p. 1)

Certainly the highest of standards is reserved for the teacher-student relationship, and it is always shocking when it is violated by school employees acting violently toward youngsters under their supervision.

How School Employees Violate Students

Two primary abusive actions define the way in which people working in schools violate students: through physical abuse and through sexual assault. There are other destructive behaviors that school officials use in relating to students that will also be mentioned within this chapter; however, excessive corporal punishment and sexual abuse and harassment will merit the greatest attention.

Excessive Corporal Punishment

Although judged less and less desirable as an appropriate disciplinary action, school officials generally have the right to use corporal punishment as a means of maintaining school discipline (unless forbidden by state law or local policy). However, when that punishment is excessive or abusive, it is violative and the teacher or administrator who delivers it can be liable for suit.

An Oklahoma superintendent, for instance, who while intoxicated spanked and beat a 10-year-old with unnecessary force was found to have violated state civil statutes protecting children from injury in such instances. There are numerous other examples from legal suits to demonstrate when school employees have used excessive force to subdue or discipline a youngster. A teacher of 230 pounds picked up a 14-year-old boy of less than half his weight and dropped him on the ground, fracturing his arm, for disregarding his instructions. Another sent his student to a hospital for several hours after battering his nose and bruising his eye. These teachers were both judged as going far beyond the reasonable force necessary to either discipline the student or protect themselves (Henderson, Golanda, & Johnson, 1989).

Parent and other advocacy groups concerned about potential violence in the use of corporal punishment, psychological scarring, and the ineffectiveness of physical force as a deterrent to unacceptable behavior have used abuse-reporting laws to pressure school officials to stop this form of discipline. In Florida, for example, some administrators who have excessively punished students physically have found themselves reported as child abusers and will be entered on an abuse registry if the report is confirmed. Harming schoolchildren through excessive physical force hurts everyone; it must stop.

Preventing Excessive Corporal Punishment

A good place to start in preventing injury from violent corporal punishment is to do away with corporal punishment as a disciplinary measure in the schools. Although such a decision will not entirely eliminate the chance of a child being physically abused by a school employee, it will help considerably. Other significant methods of prevention are listed below.

Exposing the Unspoken

Too often, there is a conspiracy of silence in a school or school district to cover up abusive behavior of colleagues or employees. Like dysfunctional families, staff members deny a problem, unwilling to admit that something is "wrong" with their school or that they could be associated with behavior that hurts children. These are situations in which responsible adults have to speak up openly and courageously to protect children, regardless of the cost. In most instances, it is a mandated duty.

Focusing on the Goals and Purposes of Schooling

School staffs that have a vision of respect and a shared system of beliefs and values regarding schools and children (refer to Chapter 2 for a discussion of these concepts) put children first. If a school or school district lives its purpose of producing whole, healthy, achieving youngsters consistently in all its professional actions, it is unlikely to also produce physically abusive employees. However simple that axiom sounds, it works.

Emphasizing Professional and Caring Behavior

Keeping the emphasis on the development of professional, caring employees whose objective it is to create independent, self-disciplined students will eventually eliminate those with violent propensities. Screen potential employees with careful scrutiny, looking for those who bring skills and strategies for building self-discipline among students and who practice constructive and positive means of disciplining students. Deal directly and firmly with employees who do resort to physical force. Where people working in schools stay in touch with their professional purposes, they do not fall into the trap of overinvolvement with students, which can sometimes cause them to behave like overwrought parents.

Sexual Abuse and Harassment

Undoubtedly among the harms that can befall a student, one of the greatest betrayals of violence from a teacher or administrator is that of sexual assault or rape. Despite how outrageous such actions are, they are not uncommon according to court cases, research studies, and anecdotal records documenting sexual assaults of students by school employees.

Federal Cases

Recently, two federal cases have sent a clear message to school officials that it will be risky to ignore complaints of sexual misconduct involving school employees and students. In a fairly recent Pennsylvania case, a young woman claimed that the school district had a constitutional duty to protect her from the sexual advances of her band instructor. When the United States Supreme Court ordered the 3rd Circuit Court of Appeals to rehear the case, *the new ruling was that school administrators could be held liable for the actions of the offending teacher because they have direct supervisory control over that teacher's actions.*

Of even greater importance was the decision of the Supreme Court itself in *Franklin v. Gwinnett County Public Schools* (1992), in which a teacher/coach subjected a student continually to harassment and coercive sex without intervention from the school authorities. The Court found that student plaintiffs can bring such suits for monetary damages against school officials under Title IX of the Education Amendments of 1972, opening the possibility of a $6 million recovery. Until this case, it had not been believed that monetary damages could be recovered under Title IX; the decision added support and impetus to the press against sexual harassment.

Forms of Sexual Harassment

The two major cases above involved high school girls who, although their complaints were ignored by school officials, at least were old enough to articulate to someone what they were experiencing. There are examples, among the numerous cases of student sexual assaults, of school personnel molesting elementary schoolchildren as young as 5 years of age. In the case of younger children, or students of any age for that matter, the offensive behavior is not always as grave as coercive sex. Sometimes it consists of fondling, indiscreet touching, vulgar language, or showing sexually explicit photographs or magazine pictures, as examples. School employees have also been reported to intimidate or threaten students into going along with their assaultive behavior out of fear of repercussions. Using their legitimate power over students to intimidate them, they threaten to lower their grades, to fail them, to belittle them, to embarrass them before their peers, or to harm them further.

Preventing Sexual Abuse and Harassment

No form of violent behavior in schools is more readily swept under the rug than that of sexual harassment and abuse. The silence that accompanies it takes the form of a conspiracy in which both perpetrator and victim participate. The perpetrator acts out of self-protection; the victim, out of fear, shame, and guilt; the school community, out of denial. To prevent sexual abuse and harassment, then, a school or school district needs to adopt the following practices.

Break the Silence

a. Make known to the school community that there are open channels of communication through which a victim can complain and be heard, without embarrassment or retaliation.
b. Set procedures for pursuing a complaint in board policy. (It is required of every Minnesota school district to have a sexual harassment policy in place from kindergarten on.)

   c. Report all suspected child abuse to the appropriate authorities.

Face the Issue Directly

   a. Discuss the characteristics of sexual abuse and harassment in faculty meetings and seminars.

   b. Invite social services representatives to participate in these discussions.

   c. Alert parents to symptoms and characteristics of abuse and harassment.

   d. Train school employees to censure the simplest forms of sexual harassment directed toward students—crude sexist jokes, suggestive looks, teasing invitations.

   e. Train employees to censure peer harassment that occurs in their presence.

   f. Take a stand on teachers dating students, recognizing that school employees maintaining sexual relationships with students are likely to be committing rape, even when the relationship is mutual.

   g. Remind staff members to be cautious about driving students home or about placing themselves in potentially compromising positions.

   h. Know and disseminate the information that sexual harassment is a power issue and that it is defined as "unwelcome sexual attention that the victim is unable to stop."

Act on (Alleged) Occurrences

   a. Investigate all complaints of sexual harassment or assault; factually document information.

   b. Involve the Personnel Department and other appropriate supervisors when it is clear that an assault has taken place; determine the next step to be taken and be aware of due process provisions.

   c. Remember that both the alleged victim and the accused have a right to protection; handle investigations and confrontations professionally, with confidentiality and with full knowledge of the rights, particularly those of privacy and due process, of both victim and the accused.

   d. Get assistance and advice from the school district's attorney.

   e. In the aftermath, pursue whatever counseling or other related services are available for the victim or victims; cooperate with any guardian "ad litem" or victims assistance program that may be available to the victim through community services.

   f. Be prepared for other alleged victims to come forward and for fact-finding as their complaints are received.

   g. Keep the staff and entire school community apprised of what steps are being taken and what information can be shared.

   h. Do not settle for an employee's resignation in lieu of pursuing an investigation or moving for dismissal where the evidence warrants.

A Word on Outsider Violence

A guidebook on violence in the schools would not be complete without a brief discussion of the violent acts that have been and seem destined to continue to be perpetrated on students *and* school employees by outsiders. In some sense, to certain individuals determined to spend their private rage and anger by lashing out indiscriminately at "society," schools have become an "attractive nuisance." Schools are filled with children, vulnerable, often powerless, many times needy, and ripe for victimization. And schools are generally quite accessible. Consequently, youngsters are beaten, shot, stabbed, raped, kidnapped, sold drugs, molested, and otherwise traumatized in the school building or on school grounds across the country, by private parties who have no association with the school organization. Adults in the school environment have also been harmed, sometimes even fatally, at the hands of strangers or individuals who knew them and intended to harm them.

When school officials are totally unaware of impending danger to a student or an employee, they cannot be held responsible for such actions taken by third parties—for a drug addict intruding into a classroom where a teacher is alone, beating her unconscious and stealing her purse, for instance. It is when administrators know or reasonably should have known of the potential for violent acts and fail to do something to decrease the possibility that they become liable. However, liability should not be the only concern of the responsible, caring educator. Doing the right thing for everyone under their supervision to the extent that they are able is the more acceptable educational standard.

Whether the potential violence is threatened by an outside party or by someone who lives in the school environment, the measures and guidelines to follow when a violent incident has occurred that are discussed in the violence category and crisis chapters will reduce both the likelihood of violence in school and the trauma of the aftermath.

In Summary

It is expected by parents and the community that teachers and administrators who, in law, have a supervisory duty over schoolchildren will exercise reasonable care in carrying out that duty. When a person working in the schools betrays that trust willfully and in complete disregard for the vulnerability of a student, especially by violent actions towards that student, the violence is all the more egregious. Each time the least form of disrespect from a school official toward a student is tolerated or ignored, the potential for larger and graver violence against students grows.

Strategies: The Roadmap to Violence Prevention

There is no reason to believe that the social, economic, political, and cultural conditions that have made violence a part of the lives of Americans, whether experienced personally or vicariously, will disappear in the near future. Realizing that some students and adults who work in the school will continue to bring attitudes that breed violence with them each day, school officials have to move toward creating a climate that neutralizes and dissipates that condition. It does not follow, however, that it is their task *alone*. Therefore, in discussing strategies for designing a safer school environment, we encourage administrators to reach out to the whole community to share responsibility for its implementation and success. As Malcolm Katz (1991) suggests, the school cannot and should not take on what are basically societal issues single-handedly. Schools must be brokers and bridge makers to other agencies—health services, social services, welfare agencies—to get interagency collaboration in reducing and minimizing the presence of violence in the school setting.

Preventing Violence in the Schools

Here we address major sources of conflict and potential violence individually, focusing on student-to-student violence because of its prevalence. The recommendations expressed here are the basis for confronting any type of violence in the schools. We offer preventive measures and strategies that have emerged from both research and practice.

Racial and Ethnic Group Conflict

One obvious but highly important characteristic of racial and ethnic conflict is prejudice. Ethnic prejudice and racism are present potentially in schools across the country wherever the school population is heterogeneous. Usually it is expressed subtly until some eruption takes place. Once the escalating signs have begun, however, school administrators are more likely to be occupied with diffusing tensions than with prevention.

It is important, therefore, to anticipate early signs of racial and ethnic conflict and to take preventive actions. These escalating signs were described by Allport in 1958 as five degrees of progressively more negative behavior:

1. Sharing prejudicial attitudes and feelings with like-minded peers
2. Avoiding contact, even totally withdrawing from contact, with certain ethnic or racial groups (turf is established; intercommunication is cut off)
3. Discriminating against ethnic and racial minority groups by exclusion from certain social functions
4. Physical attacks
5. Extermination (Sherman, 1990)

Some ways of dealing with conflict once it is in motion are discussed in the next chapter, but here we focus on what can be done to minimize it ahead of time.

The prevention of racial and ethnic conflict in schools and school districts needs to begin the first day that a student enters the classroom and to end on graduation day. A school has an opportunity to minimize intergroup conflict in the building when it provides:

- A consistent program of *curriculum development and delivery of courses* designed to encourage better race and ethnic relations and to lead to better understanding among the groups.
- Opportunities for students and staff to *openly discuss issues* of prejudice and racial or ethnic conflict.
- Opportunities for *opening and maintaining channels of communication,* thereby working on building a critical mass of trust.
- Means through which intergroupings of students can gain the *skills of group dynamics and of conflict resolution.*
- The *fostering of positive attitudes* about each other, and the encouragement to talk freely about issues in guided discussions that focus on common values such as democracy, fairness, and honesty (After King Verdict, 1992).
- *Classroom instruction,* both as part of regular subject areas (e.g., social studies) or electives (e.g., law-related education), *that confronts stereotyping.* Minorities in schools are highly sensitive to being "put down" and are aware of being treated as though they are less valued than the majority students.
- A proactive, ongoing attempt to *reach out to the minority parents and community* in ways that overcome parental reluctance and improve communication (e.g., meeting on "neutral turf") (After King Verdict, 1992).

It has to be acknowledged that the celebration of diversity and multiculturalism within schools, while contributing to the development of positive attitudes, cannot by itself resolve fears and prejudices that are born of irrationality. A proactive program of education and cross communication is necessary to counteract bias.

A Promising Example of Race Conflict Prevention

At Wilson High School, in Washington, DC, students participate in a class referred to as a "prejudice reduction workshop." Its intended purpose is to teach students, through discussion of their own experiences with prejudice as well as through other strategies, how to combat it in their school and improve race and ethnic relations. The majority of Wilson High School students are black, but there is also a percentage of white students, and over 60 countries are represented by their student body.

The workshop class is run by an organization called the Center for Dispute Settlement. As another part of the program, a corps of students have been trained to be workshop leaders themselves, enabling more and more students to participate. Actually, dispute-mediation programs of varying kinds are appearing in schools throughout the entire country. In focusing on the misunderstandings that young people have about race and ethnicity, they learn the harm that comes from racist jokes, ethnic slurs, snubbing, ridiculing, and other demeaning behaviors, and have an opportunity, in a safe setting, to empathize with each other.

Hate Crimes as Signs of Intergroup Conflict

In recent years, the presence of "hate crimes" on college and school campuses has made the headlines. These occurrences are manifestations of prejudice against and hatred of certain groups or individuals, not only because of their race or national origin but also because of their religion, sexual preference, or other distinctive characteristics. In November 1989, it was reported that a survey on incidents reflecting racial hatred (i.e., hate crimes) in schools showed that such incidents had occurred in more than one-third of the Los Angeles public schools. The typical incidents were racial slurs, name-calling, graffiti, and physical confrontations (Schmidt, 1989), but distribution of racist literature, fighting, waving of Confederate flags, and the use of guns, knives, and other weapons also occurred.

Such incidents, of course, do not happen only in large, urban school districts; they have been reported across the country. Their prevention can be approached through the same preventive strategies listed in the earlier section Racial and Ethnic Group Conflict. In planning and using preventive strategies, it is important to remember these points:

1. The earlier preventive strategies are employed, the better; children pick up biases at a very early age, and the lower elementary grades are where to start.

2. Many organizations, such as the Anti-Defamation League of B'Nai B'rith in New York and the National School Safety Center in California, have curriculum materials and other resources to help a school plan its program of prejudice reduction.

3. Proactive is better than reactive; therefore, student access to training in negotiating rather than fighting, peer mediation, and cooperation is a small investment for a school compared to the harm that anger and hatred out of control can reap.

These and other preventive measures are particularly important in regard to hate crimes, because the courts have shown great reluctance in banning offensive student "hate speech" for First Amendment reasons. An even more important reason is that hate crime, when it erupts, is extremely violent and on the rise (Bodinger-de Uriarte, 1991).

Guns and Other Weapons in Schools

What starts as two students shoving each other around can turn into a death or serious injury today, because more students are carrying weapons to school than they ever have before. Administrative anxiety regarding this fact sometimes leads to measures that arouse concerns about students' rights, and even constitutional issues. A school crackdown where there is fear that students are carrying weapons can range from the use of metal detectors to random searches of lockers, mass searches of students and of their property, and an increase in security personnel. These actions have implicit in them questions regarding the Fourth Amendment— protections against unreasonable searches that students have under the Constitution. The courts are increasingly sympathetic with the difficult circumstances under which schools labor, but they do censure gross violations of an individual's rights where there has not been reasonable cause. Therefore, school administrators need to know what those rights are and when their preventive measures violate them.

When there is clearly a need for a tough response to a threatening situation in a school, administrators must expel students possessing weapons, affirmatively search for weapons reasonably suspected to be present, use metal detectors, prosecute trespassers, and closely monitor student activity and behavior. However, a greater range of preventive strategies is needed than just those that involve sweep searches to keep weapons out of schools. Here are some suggested strategies:

- *Call together a group,* including teachers, other school personnel, parents, community representatives, perhaps other service agency people, and particularly students, to study and recommend how weapons can be kept out of the school. Students "themselves know their environment in a way no adult does, and they're in a position to make invaluable suggestions," says one wise superintendent of schools (Helgeson, 1989, p. 6A).
- Write and implement *firm policies on the consequences of carrying guns* and other weapons to school; the National School Boards Association in Alexandria, Virginia, is an excellent source of sample district policies.
- Include within the school curriculum *a handgun violence prevention program,* such as the one available from the Center to Prevent Handgun Violence in Washington, DC; incorporate into social studies classes materials and instruction on the responsibilities of the Second Amendment right to bear arms.
- *Train teachers in defusing* potentially dangerous and hostile situations and in what to do when they cannot be contained. Include in the training the appropriate language for preventing and defusing violence in the classroom and school building (Houston & Grubaugh, 1989).
- Prepare and disseminate *an emergency plan* for the school, defining roles and responsibilities.
- *Train student mediators to assist* in defusing hostile situations.
- Consider *a police department security audit* to assure a safe and secure school environment.

- Recognizing that abusive drug behavior heightens the violent behavior of those who use drugs, *be diligent in discovering drugs on campus* and work for legislation that establishes drug-free school zones.
- Carrying a weapon, and a gun particularly, can be a symbol of power, status, and intimidation for today's youngster. A constructive way to help reduce the need for raw power symbols is to *address the absence of self-esteem* that that behavior often signals. A school culture of respect for learning, life, and each other and caring adults have made differences in some youngsters' lives.

Gang Activity in Schools

There is no question that gang activity is not just an urban issue anymore; gangs appear in suburban and small town school systems, also. For suburban schools, the appearance of a gang often occurs as a result of transfer students from the city who are marginally familiar with gang paraphernalia and desperate to impress new peers.

A sociologist researching gangs says that attempting to suppress gang activity will not solve the problem, because gang membership often offers acceptance and fills a vacuum in a youngster's life. In the instance of gangs, prevention is more closely related to helping youngsters experience success in school and to providing training programs and jobs. To do that, communitywide efforts are required; collaboration among numbers of agencies such as social services, schools, police, juvenile justice officials, community groups, health services, and businesses is essential. Meanwhile, there are specific things that a school itself can do to save the marginal student who hangs at the edge, and who is especially vulnerable to gang involvement:

- Provide an after-school program and sports programs for vulnerable youngsters; seek them out, and attract them in.
- Design a program to welcome and acclimate transfer students.
- Provide appropriate role models.

- Develop a program of career counseling for the students (Moriarity & Fleming, 1990).

At the same time, programs that develop awareness of gangs for students, and provide training for staff, will strengthen the whole school's ability to cope with emerging gang activity. Finally, schools and school districts have a powerful and relatively untapped strategy available to them in combatting gangs and serving marginal youngsters generally by reaching out to other community agencies and enterprises and becoming partners. A promising concept that requires a number of collaborators is the *full-service school.*

The Full-Service School

For many reasons related to children who are at risk of failure and/or of being violently harmed, the "one-stop," *full-service school* that provides services delivered comprehensively by a number of agencies, preferably in one physical location, is a best possible prevention. A team of service providers, collaborating together to meet the special needs of poor, neglected, isolated, unsuccessful, or culturally deprived youth, has a better chance of reducing the attraction and notoriety of gang symbols and gang "brotherhood."

School district administrators, wanting to initiate a full-service program or school in their district, can look to models such as the New Beginnings program in Los Angeles or simply can begin to meet with community agencies to identify ways in which efforts affecting youngsters can be coordinated. Many states, such as Florida, are beginning to make incentive grant monies available for collaborative ventures between schools and other agencies serving at-risk children. Such initiatives can prevent broader problems than gang activity and can contribute generally to the reduction of violence in schools. Some full-service ventures offer services that range from training for parents to teenage pregnancy clinics, day care, health services, extended-day programs, tutoring, and drug-abuse assistance.

Constructive attempts to meet the needs of at-risk youngsters will be much more effective over the long haul in reducing the growth of gang membership, but there are also short-term measures that have to be taken when gang activity is occurring. To begin with, school staffs cannot bury their heads in sand. If gangs are functioning, people working in schools need to recognize the signs. Administrators, particularly, have to know of potential conflict between gang members, to prevent school incidents or to mediate them. Learn to recognize gang symbols, colors, and insignia. It is helpful also to work with the police for insight into the level of activity occurring in the community; it will ultimately impact the school.

Self-Inflicted Violence

It is a rare school or school district today that has not been touched in some way by the self-inflicted violence of the suicide of one of its students or persons working in the schools. The sudden loss of someone who belongs to the school community can have a devastating and far-reaching effect. Recognizing that such a tragedy can strike at any time, the school administrator needs to have strategies already outlined to deal with such a crisis, in order to prevent further trauma and tragedy. The preventive strategies discussed below focus on the situation where a suicide has occurred, but they are appropriate also for any violent loss, self-inflicted or not.

Staff Collaboration

As a faculty, spend in-service time learning about the grieving process and the impact of loss on individuals and a community, especially a school filled with young people. Determine steps to be taken from the moment an incident is known until the healing process is well under way. Recognize that as part of grief, there will be denial, anger, blaming, and recrimination ("If I had only done this, or that"; "I should have listened, or been there for them"), guilt, *fear*, and a myriad of intense emotions that can become epidemic and dangerous, if there is not a response. Plan a response.

Planned Interventions

Line up the interventions in advance, so they can be deployed immediately. How will the school community be informed? What are the most appropriate means of communication that will keep rumors and horror stories to a minimum? What counseling interventions will occur? Who will do them? Where will the counseling occur? How will it occur? For example, the opportunity for students to meet in relatively small groups (5 to 10) with a trained person who is able to assist them in expressing their feelings, fears, and reactions fairly soon after the tragedy can be very effective.

Assigned Tasks

Agree, before tragedy strikes, who will fulfill what tasks—of communication, counseling, dealing with the school community, the larger community, and the survivors, the funeral, and the assessment of how well the situation was handled.

Sexual Assault, Student-to-Student

The occurrence of sexual assault in schools is more thoroughly discussed in Chapter 4; however, because it happens student-to-student, it deserves mention here also. Kinds of assaults range from sexually harassing "dirty jokes" to rape, and their occurrence in schools has been documented through research studies and court cases.

The victim is much more frequently a female, but male students have also been victims. High school girls are pulled into boys' locker rooms and harassed or dragged into isolated spaces and raped; a mentally retarded student is sexually assaulted by peers in an auto body shop classroom area; two middle school girls' breasts are fondled on the school bus. Some of these incidents end up in court, with the school district and school officials as defending parties. Meanwhile, they cause the victims suffering on a continuum from embarrassment to psychological devastation and serious physical injury. Sometimes as a direct result, victims overwhelmed with shame take their lives.

There are many preventive measures that can be taken to decrease instances of sexual assault and harassment in the school setting. Some of these are described below.

Supervision

An implemented plan of building supervision based on an assessment of isolated or potentially dangerous areas around the school, as well as letting parents and students know when and where supervision is being provided, is a start. In addition, having a policy of *reacting quickly* to complaints or knowledge of sexually harassing incidents will keep those situations contained.

Education

A policy that condemns sexual harassment in school settings and supports the students' right to privacy is important. The school district or school could begin by providing education regarding the socially structured inequality between women and men (and therefore boys and girls) and the interrelationship between sex and violence. Grounding these lessons in fairness, equity, and justice would make them appropriate in social studies classes or student leadership seminars. Also, consider rape-education seminars, beginning in elementary schools. Local mental health service agencies may be able to assist schools in this regard.

Appropriate Counseling

When dating violence is confided by students to staff members, counseling for the students is necessary. There is some evidence to indicate that violence can be part of the high school dating relationship and that the victims sometimes confide this to counselors or teachers. Although severe assaults occur in relatively few dating cases, pushing, slapping, punching, and kicking happen more often (Burcky, Reuterman & Kopsky, 1988). Staff members must be able to advise and assist victims in taking the steps they need to take in order to break the association of violence with dating. Further, establishing self-help groups and providing self-esteem development through the counseling department will contribute to breaking down destructive behavior.

Potential Liability of School Employees

Sexual assault of a student by another student can involve the potential for school employee liability, depending to a large extent on whether or not the employee knew or reasonably should have known of the potential or impending danger. Schools where assaults have happened prior to the incident at hand, or where students have been threatened and school authorities know of threats or intimidation or know of a student's assaultive propensities, have often been found to have a duty to act to prevent harm.

Courts have acknowledged the responsibility of educators, generally, for safe schools and for protecting innocent students from the fear of violence. Although people working in schools are not liable as a matter of law each time a student harms another student, there are *expectations for reasonable care*. If an educator is able to *foresee potential harm to a student, that person has a legal duty of care to act to prevent it.*

Teasing, Bullying, and Victimization

Bullying and intimidating among schoolchildren is not uncommon in schools, and there is a tendency to accept it as part of "the way children are." Bullying (or harassment) can refer to physical violence against someone weaker or smaller as well as to mental violence through social isolation and exclusion. Some children are bullied and teased throughout their entire school careers, causing them to be depressed, to have low self-esteem, and eventually to drop out. Sometimes teasing and bullying have racial and ethnic or socioeconomic overtones.

School personnel rarely intervene in this activity, and bullied children are reluctant to complain or to appear as weak or as crybabies. Proactive preventive measures directed at bullying and victimization behavior among students can nip violent propensities in the bud very early on in a child's life. That is a powerful reason for people working in schools to make a strong commitment to the prevention of this kind of behavior. How can this underrated problem be reduced? Here are two suggestions.

Bullies Are Often Underachievers

The heavy emphasis on academic competition in schools exacerbates the bully's ability to gain legitimate academic respect. Ability grouping, of course, compounds the insult. Attention to individual needs, cooperative learning and group projects, and opportunities for every child to have legitimate status and success would help immensely.

Start With Intervention

Beginning with adult and student awareness of intimidation is a place to start. Awareness of the seriousness of bullying and intimidating behavior can be developed through instructional units and training seminars. There are many fine materials and resources available through conflict resolution and nonviolent behavior institutes and associations. Such organizations can provide trainers, videotapes, workshops, and seminars, or school districts can develop their own materials that assist students, teachers, and administrators to reflect on their attitudes and behavior in regard to victimization. Through these materials, students can learn to communicate calmly with each other and to articulate what is upsetting them, and thus they can have an opportunity to work toward a peaceful solution, in a safe setting, with a facilitator (Smith, 1992). Bullying is serious enough to warrant the expense of such training.

In Summary

We have offered a host of practical suggestions here. Take these recommendations for the general prevention of violence and the specific, common trouble areas as a basis for your own program. Capture the spirit of these strategies and modify them to fit your own situation. A full and effective violence prevention program is multifaceted—it starts, as we have seen, with self-examination and extends to community outreach and relationships. At any given moment, there is something that can be done toward preventing violence in schools. You can start today.

When a Crisis Happens

Prevention is the best policy, but sometimes the tensions among students and staff prove too much for even the best preventive measures and violence erupts. Even though the ideal situation is for careful policies to eliminate violent outbursts in the schools, school officials must be prepared to handle a variety of possible occurrences. The following recommendations cover the most frequent types of incidents among students, but the suggestions can be applied to any type or category of violent behavior in schools. Additional suggestions for specific cases can be found in Chapters 2, 3, and 4.

When a Racial/Ethnic Incident Actually Occurs

There are at least a dozen steps to take toward restoring order when racial/ethnic tension erupts among students in the school environment.

1. *Respond immediately* at the first flash point of an "ordinary, everyday" harassment that occurs between two or three students to avoid further escalation, and before it triggers

extraordinary events that become riotous or gravely dangerous (stabbings, shootings, etc.); passive behavior at this juncture is deadly.

2. *Anticipate escalation*, especially if the community has a history of racial or ethnic hostilities, or if the school has not dealt with such incidents directly or adequately in the past, or if there is a high tolerance of verbal or physical aggression, *or if* during such incidents, students watch but don't intervene (help defuse) or encourage and admire the perpetrators in the event (Troyna & Hatcher, 1991). These are indicators that cannot be ignored.

3. *Acknowledge when the problem is racial or ethnic* and begin working toward a resolution. If there is an escalating incident, *activate a "first response" team* that has been trained in crisis prevention or is able to handle emergencies requiring medical aid and/or crowd control.

4. *Follow ALREADY FORMULATED school policies* for dealing with perpetrators and procedures for supporting victims:

   a. Provide for a cooling down period.

   b. Insist on mutual respect and cooperation.

   c. Identify certain staff members to attend injured parties until medical assistance comes.

   d. Keep conflicting parties separated, isolated, and contained until the person investigating the conflict arrives.

   e. Arrange for crowd control and dispersal.

   f. Gather information concerning the conflict: witnesses and how to contact them, written descriptions of the incident, and so on; if a crime has occurred, keep the scene intact.

   g. Delegate each of these responsibilities in advance.

5. *Thoroughly investigate and question* participants and observers, so that any disciplinary action that is taken does not further fuel the problem. Administer discipline fairly, following due process provisions. Accompany fairness with firmness.

6. *Squelch rumors* and provide information to the school community and the larger community on a regular basis.

7. *Call in human relations support* and support from community agencies with training in defusing such incidents.

Provide time, places, counseling services, and other human resources to assist students and staff to express fear, concerns, and feelings.

8. *Encourage student leadership*, formal and informal, to be part of the solution.

9. Follow-up with *strategies to prevent further incidents*, including conflict resolution and peer mediation workshops.

10. *Involve parents and informal and formal community leaders*, especially those who work well with all students, throughout the process.

11. *Determine what additional protective measures or resources* need to be present in the school for an appropriate period of time following the incident to ensure safety. Such measures as metal detectors, patrolling policemen, and locked doors and gates are necessary short-term controls—when used over the long term, however, they may create as many liabilities and problems as they solve.

12. *Do not institute rules regarding critical incidents or emergencies for which there are not sufficient resources.* It sets up expectations that cannot be met and exposes the school to liability.

When a Gun or Other Weapon Is Used on a Student

Many of the measures cited under handling racial/ethnic conflicts are just as useful during other critical events and emergencies. For instance, when students harm other students (or anyone else in the school setting) with a weapon, all of the 12 steps above are appropriate to follow. In addition, school personnel will want to practice hard "lessons" learned by those who have personally gone through crises in school—such as killings, exploding bombs, armed intruders, and youngsters taken hostage. In a seminar in New York City, a group of such "crisis consultants" summarized the actions to be taken:

- Follow the emergency plan
- Arrange transportation for the students
- Deal directly with the media and the parents
- Offer counseling and outlets for grief

- Upgrade security and keep school safety as the primary issue after the incident
- Give ongoing assistance to the victim (Jennings, 1989)

School communities having experienced tragic crises have called parents in to talk through the crisis, hired security guards, accepted parents as volunteer hall monitors, added nurses and social service workers to their faculty, and not insignificantly, built in rituals to remember the anniversary of the event and the victims. Such rituals and opportunities, especially for students, to talk out feelings and begin the healing process are crucial. It is also crucial to get the school open again if it has been closed and to restore normalcy as soon as possible (Jennings, 1989).

When a Gang-Related Crisis Is Imminent

Once again, the dozen steps to follow when a racial/ethnic conflict arises are applicable in a gang-related crisis; however, where it appears that gang activity is imminent, school administrators will also want to be particularly careful that *modes of communication* have been set up in advance *among the school staff members* and that communication does not break down anywhere along the way.

First, as part of the school's emergency plan, develop a system for receiving and relaying information from students, community members, and each other concerning an impending incident and its possible dimensions, so that the school is not caught unaware. Second, involve the staff in controlling rumors, internally and externally. Third, communicate immediately with police or with other security persons and call for medical assistance, as soon as necessary.

When a Suicide Occurs

School officials will have two major concerns to address when the school community experiences the sudden loss of one of its members through suicide: the immediate grief that engulfs the environment as well as the residual effects of loss; and the concern that other students will "copycat" the behavior, putting some of them at high risk. The specific actions to be taken will be dictated by the specific circumstances (for example, if the suicide or other violent death actually occurs on school grounds; or if the incident involves more than one person, or is followed by more deaths; or if murder *and* suicide are involved). The basic steps to be taken are these:

- Notify the staff *directly*, immediately, and as accurately as possible.
- Have one spokesperson who shares information honestly and openly.
- Notify students and the school community, continuing to send brief updates home to parents.
- Anticipate the presence of the press and decide how that will be handled.
- Prepare to support staff and students who are experiencing distress.
- Make time to comfort the survivors, to make sensitive decisions regarding the funeral or memorial services and who will be in attendance, and to assist staff and students with plans to honor the victim's memory (Kelly, 1991).
- Remember, while working toward restoring normalcy, that grieving is a long process, and manifestations of it can appear considerably later.

When a Rape or Other Sexual Assault Occurs

Should one student sexually assault or rape another in the school setting, many of the actions described above regarding communications and squelching rumors, preserving the scene, and calling in the authorities apply. However, there are some further considerations involving this particular brand of violence:

1. Sexual assault and rape are violent *crimes*. School personnel must *be aware of state laws and local regulations* regarding what procedures are expected of them and what affirmative action must be taken.
2. *Rape and assault victims are not to blame, and services are available to these victims regardless of age.* Do not compound the

student victim's injuries. Be aware of the school's responsibility immediately following the incident to support and protect the student from further traumatization, which too often is continued by those who should be there to help in the aftermath.

In Summary

We have outlined above specific steps to be taken regarding specific kinds of violent behavior in the school building. Many of these steps apply to more than one type of situation, however, and there are certain concerns and actions that apply to *all* situations. When a crisis or tragedy happens in school, it is of utmost importance that the school administrators, their crisis response team, and the entire staff be able to perform the following actions:

1. Know and execute implicated state law and local board policies
2. Know whom to call immediately
3. Know whom to call after the crisis has played itself out
4. Secure the school
5. Calm the public
6. Counsel the school community through the stages of shock, grief, and/or post-traumatic stress
7. *Handle the crisis with integrity, focusing on "doing the right thing," and be prepared to deal with the political ramifications later*
8. Move on with plans for the future and with a commitment to rebuilding school climate

The greatest number of incidents of violence in schools involves students harming other students, but student-teacher and teacher-student violence also occurs. Being able to prevent this violence and to minimize its effects when it occurs is highly significant to people working in schools in meeting their responsibilities to provide a safe environment, and it is highly significant to students as a normative influence and a guaranty of the chance to learn.

7

Final Words to the School Administrator

This "get tough" attitude may help to improve school order and safety. But the reforms to date bring to mind King Canute, who tried to hold back the sea with his bucket. The most urgent and important issue—the social pathology of the communities in which these schools are located—has yet to be addressed.

(MENACKER, WELDON, & HURWITZ, 1989)

Although intended to be in part a guidebook for administrators on how to successfully defuse violent situations in schools, this book leans more heavily in the direction of preventive and interventive measures. Wishing to avoid being modern-day Canutes, or to encourage administrators to repeat the futility of King Canute's hopeless efforts to keep back the sea, we have tried often to say that get-tough strategies are important as stopgap measures and for making clear the purpose of schools to those who have forgotten. Such measures in the long run, however, will exacerbate the very problems that schools are committed to resolving.

We believe in order, discipline, learning, and schools without violence. We believe, also, with Menacker, Weldon, and Hurwitz (1989), that the road to them is through "interventions that address conditions within both the schools *and* their communities" (p. 55). *Community well-being, with healthy schools as a component, is the goal,* and more tools than a simple bucket are needed to accomplish it. Interagency collaboration, different governance structures for schools and other agencies, coordinated policies, adequate funding, and a whole host of partnerships among human services, schools, business, and government are required. The task sounds monumental, and in its entirety, it is. However, remembering that the road to success is built piece by piece, one school or one school district could begin the cycle by practicing some of the preventions and interventions recommended throughout this book. Ultimate success will depend on the attitudes, aspirations, and actions of the given school or school district.

Powerful Attitudes

There is significant power in the values, beliefs, and attitudes of an organization. We all know success stories of schools that operate under the most difficult and sometimes violent of situations. Led by a principal, or an entire staff, or even a community that believes in their children and themselves, certain schools perform against great odds. What is it that makes those successes possible? Our hunch is that the reasons are integrally connected to constructive attitudes about schools, children, and themselves. To put energy into achieving a violence-free school, people working in the school would have to accomplish the following:

- Respect the school's youngsters as valuable and worth extraordinary effort
- Value teaching and learning strongly
- Have a student focus
- Believe that risk factors with which children come to school can be mitigated
- Have confidence that their efforts could make a difference

- Trust each other to get the job done
- Believe they are making a contribution that counts
- Believe that they would be supported
- Be willing to share, release turf, and become interdependent
- Be inclusive, not exclusive
- Be willing to take risks
- Be an integral part of the school community
- Be committed to doing the right thing

Proactive Actions

The measures we have recommended for defusing and preventing violence imply proactivity. The encroachment of violence on a school building or a school system demands consistent and continuous acts that are intended to restore or keep what makes learning possible—a safe, orderly, and healthy school environment. *Proactivity that benefits children implies a plan for action that is both bold and thoughtful.* The plan, to make educational sense, has to be based on the vision and articulated mission of the school community. If school employees respond to violence with the overzealousness of a Joe Clark, the mission of the institution and the values that educators commonly hold are washed away.

Potent Aspirations

Many of the preventive measures we are recommending have in them the seeds of expansive programs and projects—from violence prevention programs to full-service schools and interagency collaboration. These require creative efforts to find financial support (perhaps grants), to receive waivers of local and state regulations, to discover new resources, and to use staff in new and different ways. School administrators wanting to employ interventions to make a school's environment more safe and productive will be successful in those efforts. Don't go it alone. Create task forces and interdisciplinary teams to go with you. Remember that aspirations to stop individuals within and outside of the school community from hurting the members of that community, so that those members can learn and live productively, are potent. This is not an overnight project.

The Big Picture

School employees working in their schools and school districts to prevent violence are connected, knowingly or unknowingly, to concurrent efforts on the local, state, and federal levels. There are indicators every day of groups and coalitions forming on all levels to defuse and prevent the growing violence that impacts schools. California has been in the forefront in guaranteeing through legislative provisions that safe schools are a student's inalienable right. Minnesota is going all out to attack violence from the state level, providing 25% of Head Start's annual budget in the state and getting behind numbers of antiviolence grass-roots projects. There are many other examples. In all, there is definitely an affirmative push from many corners to support local school administrators in their efforts to proactively defuse and prevent violence. We *can* do more than just cope.

Annotated Bibliography and References

Albee, G. W., Bond, L. A., & Cook Monsey, T. V. (Eds.). (1992). *Improving children's lives: Global perspectives on prevention*. Newbury Park, CA: Sage.

This edited book of writings by an international team of scholars, practitioners, educators, and policymakers from multiple countries analyzes common problems in promoting the healthier development of children. Each of the articles is instructive, but of primary interest to the topic of this book are: Huckleberry Finn and street youth everywhere: an approach to primary prevention; Television violence: A proactive prevention campaign; Victimization against schoolchildren: Intervention and prevention; and Infecting our children with hostility.

Barish, S., Excell, M. T., & Coonan, J. S. (1991). I was there when tragedy struck. *The School Administrator, 48*(5), 12-14, 16-17.

Three administrators describe how they coped when tragedies struck their schools, the roles they played, and the emotions with which they were forced to deal.

Crewdson, J. (1988). *By silence betrayed: Sexual abuse of children in America*. Boston: Little, Brown.

A Pulitzer Prize-winning journalist gives startling and significant information about the extent of child abuse in this country and suggests what can be done to stem its growth.

Donnellan, A. M., LaVigna, G. W., Negri-Shoultz, N., & Fassbender, L. (1988). *Progress without punishment: Effective approaches for learners with behavior problems.* New York: Teachers College Press.

The authors present constructive intervention strategies for learners with severe behavior problems in a practical format for staff who work regularly with such student problems. The legal and administrative issues related to positive programming are also discussed.

Dziech, B. W., & Weiner, L. (1990). *The lecherous professor: Sexual harassment on campus.* Urbana: University of Illinois Press.

Although this book addresses college campus issues, it has an extremely well written definition of sexual harassment and a clear description of how certain teachers use the academic setting to seduce their students.

Elders, M. J. (1992). School-based clinics to the rescue. *The School Administrator, 49*(8), 16-18, 20-21.

This article describes how a number of school districts are beginning to offer school-based health services, how that can be done with minimal risk, and what partners can be pulled in to assist in the effort.

Fertman, C. I. (1992). Establishing a school-community agency collaboration. *NASSP Practitioner, 19*(1), 1-8.

School administrators and superintendents interested in developing collaborative efforts with other human service agencies will find this pamphlet an informative starting place.

Gittins, N. E. (Ed.). (1988). *Fighting drugs in the schools: A legal manual.* Alexandria, VA: National School Boards Association.

Discusses the legal constraints that have to be taken into consideration when schools and school districts wage a war on drugs.

Grossnickle, D. R. (1989). *Helping students develop self-motivation: A sourcebook for parents and educators.* Reston, VA: National Association of Secondary School Principals.

A good, short sourcebook for beginning the process of helping students build motivation and experience success.

Hate crime: A sourcebook for schools confronting bigotry, harassment, vandalism, and violence. Published by the Southwestern Regional Laboratory.

This sourcebook includes a curriculum planning guide, a checklist to help determine whether a specific incident constitutes a hate crime, a school survey for assessment of the presence of hate crimes, and other information. It is written for both school and school district personnel and includes listings of other resources. Copies may be obtained from Research for Better Schools, 444 North Third Street, PA 19123.

Jehl, J., & Kirst, M. (1992). Spinning a family support web among agencies, schools. *The School Administrator, 49*(8), 8-13, 15.

The changes that will be required of school officials as school districts begin to link with health and social services are discussed. A very successful pilot program in San Diego is highlighted.

Kelley, E. A. (1980). *Improving school climate: Leadership techniques for principals.* Reston, VA: National Association of Secondary School Principals.

A guidebook for administrators on how to go about building a vital school climate and how to recognize the elements of a healthy school climate.

Levy, A. (1989). *Focus on child abuse: Medical, legal and social work perspectives.* Hampshire, Great Britain: Hawksmere, Ltd.

Interesting collection of essays by human service providers in England dealing with child abuse. Good comparative information with which to see a total picture. Also, a helpful article on a model for interagency collaboration in regard to child sexual abuse.

Morrow, G. (1987). *The compassionate school.* Englewood Cliffs, NJ: Prentice-Hall.

An invaluable practical guide to educating abused and traumatized children. Excellent materials including charts, checklists, and forms that are easily adaptable to an individual school's needs.

NASSP AP Special, VII(3), April 1992, 1-12.

A special issue of the National Association of Secondary School Principals (NASSP) newsletter for assistant principals dedicated entirely to peer mediation programs. NASSP is at 1904 Association Drive, Reston, VA 22091.

National School Safety Center. (n.d.). *The right to safe schools: A newly recognized inalienable right.* Malibu, CA: National School Safety Center.

Contact the center at Pepperdine University, Malifbu, CA 90265, to obtain this publication and a list of other available materials.

National School Safety Center. (1985). *School safety legal anthology.* Malibu, CA: Pepperdine University Press.

A thorough compilation of legal issues related to safety of importance to school administrators as well as parents.

Straight talk about risks, or STAR

> *This is a curriculum for grades K-12 on violence and guns, written by the Center to Prevent Handgun Violence, a national education and lobbying group. It contains activities regarding conflict resolutions and decision-making contributing to safety and offers a video on teenage victims of gun violence. Contact the Center to Prevent Handgun Violence, 1225 I Street, N.W., Suite 1100, Washington, DC 20005.*

Welsh, P. (1992). Young, black, male, and trapped. *Annual editions: Sociology 91/92,* pp. 37-39. Guilford, CT: Dushkin Publishing Group.

A quick glimpse into the particular problems of dealing with bias, stereotyping, and being stigmatized, which young black males experience, regardless of social or economic standing. Useful material for educators who want to understand how some of these youngsters become angry and violent.

Zuelke, D. C., & Willerman, M. (1992). *Conflict and decisionmaking in elementary schools: Contemporary vignettes and cases for school administrators.* Dubuque, IA: William C. Brown.

Intended to help elementary school administrators make better decisions and manage problem situations more successfully. Good practice exercises.

References

After King verdict and riots, educator discusses race relations. (1992, May 13). *Education Week*, pp. 6-7.

Barth, R. (1990). *Improving schools from within.* San Francisco: Jossey-Bass.

Bodinger-de Uriarte, C. (1991, December). The rise of hate crime on school campuses. *PDK Research Bulletin*, 1-6.

Burcky, W., Reuterman, N., & Kopsky, S. (1988, May). Dating violence among high school students. *The School Counselor, 34*(5), 353-358.

Flax, E. (1989, May 24). Panel hears testimony on the causes of violent acts by nation's teenagers. *Education Week*, p. 13.

Franklin v. Gwinnett County Public Schools, 112 S.Ct. 1028 (1992).

Gerl, G. (1991). Thwarting intruder violence in our schools. *NASSP Bulletin, 75*(534), 75-79.

Helgeson, M. (1989, March 8). Board tackles weapons in schools. *Education Week*, pp. 1A, 6A.

Henderson, D. H., Golanda, E. L., & Johnson, N. C. (1989). The use of force by public school teachers as a defense against threatened physical harm. 54 Ed. Law Rep. 773.

Houston, R., & Grubaugh, S. (1989). Language for preventing and defusing violence in the classroom. *Urban Education, 24*(1), 25-37.

Jennings, L. (1989, October 4). 'Crisis consultants' share lessons they learned from school violence. *Education Week*, pp. 1, 27.

Katz, M. (1991). Putting the holistic educational leadership puzzle together. *Planning and Changing, 22*(1), 13-22.

Kelly, D. G. (1991). Anatomy of a tragedy, a critique of one district's response to a crisis. *The School Administrator, 48*(5), 8-11.

Lawton, M. (1992, September 9). Study shows steep rise in juvenile violent crime. *Education Week*, p. 18.

Mawdsley, R. D. (1992, September). Sexual misconduct by school employees. *A Legal Memorandum.* National Association of Secondary School Principals, pp. 1 - 8.

Menacker, J., Hurwitz, E., & Weldon, W. (1990). Discipline, order, and safety in elementary schools. *Streamlined Seminar, 8*(4), 8.

Menacker, J., Weldon, W., & Hurwitz, E. (1989). School order and safety as community issues. *Phi Delta Kappan, 71*(1), 39-40, 55-56.

Moriarity, A., & Fleming, T. W. (1990). Youth gangs aren't just a big-city problem anymore. *The Executive Educator, 12*(7), 13-16.

Schmidt, P. (1989, November 15). "Hate crimes" are called "serious problem" in L.A. *Education Week*, p. 7.

Sherman, R. L. (1990). Intergroup conflict on high school campuses. *Journal of Multicultural Counseling and Development, 18*(1), 11-18.

Smith, S. J. (1992). How to decrease bullying in our schools. *Principal, 72*(1), 31-32.

Troyna, B., & Hatcher, R. (1991). Racist incidents in schools : A framework for analysis. *Journal of Educational Policy, 6*(1), 17-31.

Wilson, J. Q. (1992, June 10). Point of view: Scholars must expand our understanding of criminal behavior. *Chronicle of Higher Education*, p. A40.

Zirkel, P., & Gluckman, I. (1991). Assaults on school personnel. *NASSP Bulletin, 75*(533), 102-106.